People Are Social Creatures

By nature, people are social creatures needing fellow human beings, a community, to survive. The more active a person participates in society and his or her community the happier and more content that person is. People need other people. Individuals need friends and acquaintances for optimal self-fulfillment and self-realization and to experience happiness and joy. Becoming isolated from one's environment and community - from fellow human beings - results in losing the ability for self-realization and fulfillment, which is only possible within society.

Since inhibited individuals have the inner urge to isolate themselves from society and human companionship this ability to make and maintain contact with other individuals and groups, with society, has to be deliberately trained until it becomes a habitual behavior pattern. This is the purpose and objective of the 9th step. Nevertheless, we are already ahead of the game because you have mastered emotional expressiveness to the point where it has become a part of your subconscious reaction system.

Deliberately practicing social skills is also practicing courage. Courage is CONFIDENCE, GUTSINESS, PLUCK. The courage to be daring and confident of your abilities. The courage to establish free emotional contact with all people in all situations and the courage to develop freely wherever you are. These abilities are exactly the opposite of your previous inhibitions. One could also say that courage for social contact is the opposite and the non-existence of inhibitions and inhibition symptoms. And that inhibitions are the lack of a non-existence of social courage. The 9th step thus serves to practice social courage, to practice sociability and the ability to make social contact and with that the opposite of inhibitions. Practicing courage and sociability also expands your sphere of life, thus offering new and previously un- or underutilized development and self-realization opportunities.

The Multipurpose Exercise of the 9th Week

The main exercise of this 9th week consists of using every opportunity to engage in conversations, talk, and discussions and to search out social contact wherever and whenever possible. This exercise has several objectives and thus is a multipurpose exercise. It provides several positive effects as described in the following brief explanation, which will give you a better understanding of the subject:

1. Increasing the ability for uninhibited emotional expressiveness

2. Increasing social courage

3. Expanding your personal sphere of life

4. Intensifying the ability to speak and participate in discussions in a liberated emotional manner

5. Expanding your personal ability for self-fulfillment and self-development

6. Increasing sociability

7. Increasing opportunities for true happiness within and due to social contacts and social situations

8. Complete elimination of specific inhibitions and inhibition symptoms with special focus on those associated with discussions, conversations, and social contact Eliminating especially those inhibitions that used to result in xenophobia, fear conversing with others, fear of public speech, feelings of social inferiority, and lack of human contact.

This list shows that the exercises of this 9th week have an especially intensive disinhibition effect and an equally strong development fostering effect.

A varied complex effect is achieved as well, for example, the heightened expressiveness has a feedback effect on the ability for self-realization and development. More social courage results in more zest for life and more courage to face everyday situations. The newly experienced, expanded ability for self-development has a positive effect on the courage and each and every individual and partial effect thus increases and heightens other partial effects in many different ways. All of these partial effects promote the overall disinhibiting process to such an extent that the final objective and goal of the Emotional Liberation Method is within easy reach.

The main goal of this week of training is therefore to deliberately search out and utilize every opportunity of your everyday life to establish social contacts and to interact with other people. Here are some details:

- A.) No matter what the social contact situation or interaction, always express yourself completely liberated, unencumbered, and with emotional expressiveness. Actively participate in any conversation you are engaged in a liberated and emotionally involved manner. Try to become an equal partner in the conversation. Do not diminish your part in any conversation or social contact situation you are confronted with.

- B.) Deliberately search out opportunities and possibilities for participating in conversations and discussions even if you are not yet part of that conversation or situation. Be proactive! Speak active and in an emotionally liberated and animated manner and be an equal partner in the conversation.

- C.) If you do not have the opportunity to join a conversation or discussion already in progress then actively search out opportunities to start discussions and conversations yourself.

D.) Try to make new acquaintances by engaging others in conversations. Expand your personal sphere of life and circle of friends as well as your social ability to develop; include people you previously did not know at all or only knew a little. Try to engage in conversation with people you previously were afraid of or who triggered inhibition symptoms; this will increase tour personal courage!

E.) If you discover that a conversation partner has the same interest as you try to maintain contact with this person and deepen your social contact until it develops into friendship.

F.) Try to be as much among people during this week of training as possible. Avoid isolating yourself socially. This will create the foundation for social contacts wherever and whenever. Try to follow through even if this seems difficult. Your primary focus and priority for this week is:

<u>I WILL SEARCH OUT SOCIAL CONTACT WHEREVER AND WHENEVER EVEN REMOTELY POSSIBLE AND I WILL ALWAYS EXPRESS MYSELF IN AN EMOTIONAL AND LIBERATED MANNER!</u>

Implement and realize this guideline within as well as outside of your previous and current sphere of life. Try to make contact with people you do not know too well and people you do not know at all. For one week, your primary objective is to search out social contacts wherever and whenever possible and to express yourself freely and in an animated and emotional manner. This will mean a strenuous week for you, which, however, will also yield excellent results concerning your ability to establish social contact and provide you wit a new level of freedom and confidence. The positive effects and social skills and experiences acquired during this one week will contribute to your becoming socially active person. A variety of inhibitions disappear as well as feelings of inferiority and your inner attitude and social behavior will change from the ground up. After this intensive week of training and practice you will notice that your courage and your sociability have already been integrated into your new reaction system as new behavioral patterns.

Striving for an Equal Main Role

Inhibited individuals are known to be yes-men and yes-women; they agree with whatever the other person is saying. They do not dare have a different opinion due to their inhibitions. They are not EQUAL partners. Your assignment for this week of training is to be an equal partner during conversations, discussions, chats, and other social contacts. This means you are to actively participate in any conversation, freely express your emotions, and voice your own opinions even if they differ. Adjust to the respective situation. However, this also means that you freely "butt in" when others are talking, as long as you keep your manners and remain polite. Of course, do not be inconsiderate or rude.

Striving for an equal role during any conversation is so very important because inhibited individuals (even those you have already achieved a certain level of disinhibition but used to be very inhibited) always think "All or nothing!" and this attitude might result in your trying to assume the absolute main role in all of your exercises. This, however, would soon lead to disappointments and failure because anybody initiating conversations just for the purpose of playing the absolute main role, to be the sole center of attention, is not well-liked and is dejected as being selfish. And that is exactly the opposite of our objective.

This is why you have to try being an EQUAL partner and affording your opposites the same rights you claim during any conversation - and vice versa, of course. Being an equal conversation partner means to claim and take advantage of the same rights as all of the other participants; it means to freely and emotively agree or disagree, to object and even attack if warranted.

Make sure you express your opinions vivaciously and freely as well as honestly. Be as emotionally free as you have leaned to be by now. Fully apply the complete scope of what you have leaned up to now. Do not express only thoughts but also express your mood, emotions, feelings, stirrings, etc. just as well as calm concurrence. Make you express all emotions honestly and authentically. Do no limit yourself to using your speech organs alone. Speak with emphasis, with facial expressions and gestures, with your entire body. Remember: Every single expression is to be an OVERALL, TOTAL EXPRESSION of your ENTIRE personality! Any suppressed expression will cause new inhibitions. Only freely expressing your emotions - unencumbered overall expressiveness - will disinhibit and liberate you from your inhibition symptoms. This free emotional overall expressiveness has to become a habitual reaction system and behavior and speech pattern.

The Technique of Social Contact

It is easy to engage friends and good acquaintances in conversation. This does not need to be discussed in detail. However, talking with strangers or even "superiors" is often quite difficult but can be easily mastered as well if the technique of social contact is understood.

Social contact can be initiated in a variety of different ways. The easiest way is to be sensitive to the current emotions of your conversation partner. His or her current mood, feelings, and overall emotional state. This makes establishing social contact very easy. First, observe the respective person and try to detect and recognize his or hers current emotional state. Then, just start with a phrase that matches that emotional state. Here are some examples:

For example, if you see that the respective person is bored by having to wait you can say the following: *"Waiting is so tedious!"*

If a person is waiting for a train, for example, you can look at your watch and say: *"Two more minutes and the train will be here!"*

If a person is freezing says: *"Rather cold here!"* If it is warm, say: *"Rather warm here! Don't you agree?"*

Use the ambience of a restaurant for making social contact: *"It's rather busy here!"* Or *"Not much going on tonight!"*

There are many opportunities in any situation to make social contact by commenting on the current mood. The other way is to ask a question. Ask for the current time, a light for your cigarette; ask how long something will take, etc.

To participate in already ongoing conversations use the mood or thought currently expressed by one of the other participants as a "hook." Either voice agreement or disagreement. Or intervene in an ongoing conversation by expressing strong and immediate opposition to something another participant has just stated; this is especially effective if several other individuals also disagree. You can also ask a question about something another person has just expressed; ask him or her to elaborate on a statement. Or emphasize a just expressed statement by a certain facial expression or body movement such as an interested facial expression or by tilting your head to signal that you are listening, for example. If you want to be especially polite it is also possible to ask first if it is okay with the others if you "barge into" their conversation. This, however, is usually not necessary. Just start the conversation at a point someone else has stopped.

Here is a summary of possibilities of participating in conversations and chats:

1. Stay attuned to and comment on current emotional state
2. Stay attuned to and comment on just expressed thought and idea
3. Agree by expressing the same emotions
4. Agree by expressing the same idea
5. Express disagreement by expressing an opposite emotion
6. Express disagreement by expressing an opposing idea
7. Ask to be allowed to speak, draw attention to yourself
8. Politely ask to participate in the conversation
9. Ask a question about the topic being discussed
10. Draw attention to yourself by asking a question concerning a topic other than the one currently being discussed
11. Look straight at a speaking individual and use facial expressions and gestures to signal that you are deeply involved in the conversation and are keenly listening

There are thus many opportunities to participate in talks and conversations. Once initial contact has been established and the first phrase has been spoken the rest is rather easy and happens almost automatically. Many inhibited individuals shy away from participating in conversations and chats because they feel they have nothing "smart" or "significant" to contribute to a conversation. This belief completely unfounded. Conversations and chats are social contacts with a life of their own, always in flux and always changing. They do not take place on only one level where it is important that you say something "smart" or "witty". What is important, however, is that you do participate and express yourself freely, vividly, and in an emotionally authentic manner. Asking bartenders, innkeepers, or individuals working in restaurants who are privy to a great many conversations about the contents of these conversations you will discover that the majority of chats have very trivial and insignificant topics, are nothing more than chitchat about everyday things. Conversations are not for saying something "smart" or "witty" but serve to entertain, to provide pleasure and joy, to relax from stress, and last but not least for developing social skills, furthering the socialization process and to promote self-development and self-fulfillment.

Spend a night at the local inn or bar to see why conversations are so important for socialization and human interaction.

A Rational and Simple Calculation

"Time is money!" Most of you have heard this saying many times. And this is also true. Time has a value if utilized properly and fully. This means that the time you spend on training and practicing using the EL Method has a value for your future. Just think of the professional benefits of unencumbered, free expressiveness and articulateness. Professional success is based on skills and abilities that are useable and valuable for your professional development. You also need the ability to apply and utilize your skills and expertise in an optimal manner. Both of these success factors decide about the actual opportunities of any professional development and the direction a career path takes.

Many inhibited individuals have a wealth of experience and skills but these individuals are usually not able to utilize and apply these skills and abilities for their own benefit and the benefit of society as a whole because they simply lack the means to express themselves. If and when such a person with plenty of knowledge, expertise, and skills is able to use systematic and deliberate exercises to master the ability of free expression or becomes very articulate then professional unrecognized or unknown opportunities suddenly become available.

Machines and devices seem to increasingly become important but this does not mean that human communication is becoming unimportant because the people that operate these machines and devices have to be instructed and guided to make sure that these existing machines really can provide optimal benefit and efficiency for society. And that means every company and every enterprise needs people who can communicate with qualified specially trained experts as well as with the hired help. This is where being articulate and being able to express yourself freely play a decisive role. Modern operations are no longer based on physical labor of a labor force but increasingly focus on intelligent, well-trained, highly qualified personnel. If it used to be possible to manage a company with commands and strict instructions, today's personnel management requires a vast array of different skills. Modern employees are better educated and more intelligent. Employees of today's successful enterprises are no longer the quasi-servants of their all-powerful bosses and masters - eternally grateful for giving the opportunity to work long hours for little pay - but are voluntary, intelligent, independent, creative and innovative team members with the same rights and duties as their superiors.

Today, individuals are valued who are capable of working within a team and as an equal partner. Individuals who are able to manage and handle machinery as well as intelligent employees have the best promotional prospects. And free expressiveness plays a decisive role. To guide and direct employees, to convince and persuade, to be a leader and top manager requires not only expert knowledge but also the ability to express and articulate your knowledge. No matter how much of an expert someone is, the opportunities for advancement will never be as abundant as for someone who is an expert AND knows how to express himself or herself. Today's companies are looking for people who are articulate as well as skilled. People who can be entrusted with important tasks and projects, who can be counted on to prevail for the good of the whole -thanks to their expressiveness.

If you think of the time spent on these exercises over the past few weeks, it becomes clear that this time was never wasted but represents a true benefit and value for your professional development - the EL Method is an investment in your personal AND professional future. The ability to express yourself freely and truly, a high level of articulateness, are factors that benefit society as a whole as well as the individuals. In addition to specialized knowledge and professional skills, articulateness and free expression are a decisive factor determining the type of benefit and value an individual can offer society. And since remuneration is according to the benefit offered by an individual to society, this factor also decides income and the extent of participation in the prosperity and benefits society can provide in turn.

That every individual hour spent fostering and promoting your articulation and expressiveness skills will have its very specific and often tangible rewards is thus a very straightforward and logical deduction. Maybe this value cannot be expressed purely in money but we might be able to say that this value represents an intellectual investment or capital, which will yield considerable interest in the future. An intellectual capital that is not subject to devaluation or inflation.

How to Eliminate Embarrassing Moments

Inhibited individuals are not the only ones to experience embarrassing moments, pauses, or situations. The sheer multitude of daily adjustments any person has to undergo dictates that there will be unexpected, sudden events no person could ever anticipate. The first reaction to such an event is the emotion of SURPRISE. We become aware of our surprise and now have to express this emotion as well. If expressed clearly, the immediate feeling of relief is significant and allows us to think clearly again. If, however, the surprise emotion is suppressed, it soon develops into EMBARRASSMENT and INSECURITY, two rather undesirable emotions. The first step to eliminate and nullify such moments of embarrassment is thus to express the feeling of SURPRISE as freely and immediately as possible. Here are some examples: *"Oh! I did not expect that today!"* --- *"Ah! What a surprise! I did not anticipate seeing you today!"* --- *"Oh! I do not know what to say! What a surprise!"* --- *"I am speechless! This is quite unexpected!"* --- *"Oh! Excuse me! But I really was not prepared for this! I did not give this any thought at all today!"*

Moments of surprise can become complex and comprehensive inhibition symptoms with far reaching effects if they are not discharged in time through free emotional expression. Once this emotion has been suppressed, it is still possible to express this feeling of EMBARRASSMENT. This is a simple way out off the dilemma but one many people shy away from because they believe that expressing embarrassment is a weakness and disgrace. However, this is not the case in real life. A person freely and openly expressing his or her embarrassment is not considered weak or insecure - just the opposite - others think of him or her as open, honest, authentic, and even quick-witted and flexible. Such expressions of embarrassment are as follows: *"Oh no! Now I am really embarrassed!"* --- *"Well! I have no clue what to do or say! I am quite embarrassed!"* --- *"You? Here? I can't believe it! This is quite a conundrum for me!"* --- *"I do not know what to say! I am at a loss for words right now!"*

The so-called QUICK CONTACT method is a technique applied to handle sudden moments of embarrassment and consists of immediately evoking a lively emotion regardless whether this emotion makes sense or not. This lively emotion is then expressed especially vivaciously and graphically. Some exaggeration in the beginning is okay. Here are some examples: *"Oh! How pretty you have become since the last time I laid eyes on you! You are a picture of beauty - like a blooming rose!"* This can be expressed towards a woman, for example, whom a man has not seen for quite some time and who used to trigger severe inhibition symptoms. Another example: *"Well, look at you! You have changed so much! Let me have a good look at you! How handsome you have become!"* This can be expressed towards a man, for example, whom a woman has not seen for quite some time and who used to trigger severe inhibition symptoms.

These two examples clearly illustrate that instead of giving in to your own embarrassment you can embarrass the other person just a tiny little bit by freely and genuinely expressing your emotions. Once the first moment of the embarrassing situation has been handled with this quick contact method, then one word usually follows the next, and before you know it the embarrassing situation has been mastered without really exposing your embarrassment very much.

Try to use an especially lively facial expression when eliminating these types of embarrassing moments. This means expressing genuine emotion using your face. Dry and factual words do not help much in these situations. True emotional expression, however, helps a great deal. Genuine emotional expressiveness!

Here are some more examples for the quick contact technique: *"Oh no! Oh no! Oh no! YOU of all people! - I am sure you know that I do not like you all that much - but what can I do? I just have to bear it! Okay, let's get this over with - what can I do for you?"* -- - *"Ha! What do you think you're doing? How fresh can anybody be?" --- "I am amazed! Really! What a surprise! I would have never believed I would meet you again so fast after our first meeting!" --- "Man! Why did you have to frighten my like that? What are you doing here?"*

The quick contact technique consists of quickly expressing some kind of emotion in a very lively manner as soon as you become aware of the embarrassing situation. Regardless whether the expressed emotion is one of surprise, like, dislike, or any other feeling. Just expressing an emotion will imbue you with confidence and courage to handle the situation. However, wherever and whenever an emotion of surprise and embarrassment is suppressed and subsequently accumulated, inhibition symptoms occur in just a few seconds, which will make it difficult to return to free emotional expressiveness. Embarrassing moments are enemies, which can be eliminated only if attacked immediately. If given any leeway whatsoever, they will overpower and dominate you.

A common inhibition cause consists of the opinion that PERFECT and 100% PROPER reactions are absolutely required at all times. No human being is completely and always right and perfect. People just react as best as possible to situations, an environmental stimulus, or an emotion. That's all! Living means: Continuous adaptation to one's environment. And any adaptation is fraught with mistakes, which - if necessary - can then be corrected. Optimal adaptation (and with that viable and successful socialization) is only possible if mistakes that have been made are corrected. In everyday life this always means an approximate adaptation but never a perfect adaptation. This is the inhibition-causing thought pattern: *"I have to do this right! "I have to do this perfectly!"* This is nothing more than a characteristic of existing feelings of inferiority. This thought pattern usually disappears all by itself once the disinhibiting process is well on its way.

Exercise Schedule for the Ninth Week

1. Practice Establishing Social Contacts

Realize and apply the following formula during this week of training:

"I WILL SEARCH OUT SOCIAL CONTACT WHEREVER AND WHENEVER EVEN REMOTELY POSSIBLE AND I WILL ALWAYS EXPRESS MYSELF IN AN EMOTIONAL AND LIBERATED MANNER!"

This means you utilize any situation wherever and whenever possible to establish social contact with other people. Actively participate in conversations and discussions. Deliberately search out suitable situations and opportunities for social contact. Initiate conversations yourself; engage as many people as humanly possible; and always, always exercise optimal, free, genuine emotional overall expressiveness. Try to make new acquaintances and even friends. Strive for playing an equal role during any social contact. This will heighten your free emotional overall expressiveness as well as your ability for social contact and courage to establish such contact.

2. STANDARD EXMOTION EXERCISES

Once again, practice one STANDARD EXMOTION EXERCISE every day. However, if you have the opportunity to be in a larger company, then practice one additional exmotion exercise before leaving the house. You will notice that the aftereffects of the additional exmotion exercise will be especially useful in a larger group of people. You can perform such exercises also when faced with important meetings, negotiations, or other socially or professionally significant situations.
